ded★i★ca★tion -

a name and often a message prefixed to a literary, musical, or artistic production in tribute to a person or cause.

This book is dedicated to every kid who has ever attended a Power Workshop and every kid who hasn't experienced one yet. In other words, this book is for YOU.

I believe that the hope of the world has always hinged on the higher calling of young people. History shows that great civilizations have crumbled because a few greedy, selfish, and evil people had their way while the great majority were either silent, lazy, or huddled in fear.

Our hope and prayer is that you will take these messages and chase your dreams. You will always seek the truth and refuse to be just average. You will develop a passion for life and will overcome your fears with world-changing faith and belief. Run your race and be too tough to quit. Have fun while you're making this world a better place. We need you.

Top Secrets of Success...
4 Kids

(real) fun only lasts when you know the secrets...

GET REAL

Russell and Lin Jones
illustrated by Steve Nyman

Top Secrets of Success . . . 4 Kids

Published by Insight Publishing Group
8801 S. Yale, Suite 410
Tulsa, OK 74137
918-493-1718

ISBN: 1-930027-23-0
LOC NO.: 00-105280

Printed in the United States of America.

Why we wrote this book and **who** it's for:

The main mission of this book is to:

1 - show young people how each of them is special and unique.

2 - show young people how to distinguish between real dreams and fantasy.

3 - give young people a system of getting from where they are to where they want to be.

4 - bring parents (mentors) and their children (10-15 yr. olds) together in a real and meaningful way.

5 - give parents a tool to edify (build up) their children and to keep the lines of communication open.

The book will be in a format that will encourage the readers to only read a few pages per day. These pages will consist of relevant artwork (that will help the reader remember the message), text for discussion, and a positive affirmation that will further aid the reader to internalize the message.

Contents

Russell and Lin Jones

Intro
for Kids

What's the fastest way to the top of the World Trade Center? If you've seen the Power Workshop, you know the answer is the elevator. The elevators in your life are mom, dad, special teachers, pastors, ministers, rabbis, coaches, etc. These are the people in life who can help you get from where you are to where you want to be . . . faster than you can by yourself. Why? Because of wisdom and experience. Most of the time, they have already been there, done that. They know what works and if they're anything like me, they know for sure what doesn't work.

Most young people miss (or ignore) the elevators in their life and try to take the stairs to the top. Look out! There's no wisdom or experience there. There are obstacles, disasters, problems and all kinds of bad stuff you have never even thought of. People get lost on the stairs. Their friends can't help because they've never been there before either. Taking the stairs is definitely a prescription for failure. Don't miss the elevator!

This book is designed for you to read with one of your elevators (mentors). It will be a fantastic experience for both of you. Your best choice for an elevator would be mom or dad. If that's not possible, find someone else who you can trust and who has done something special with their life. Don't be afraid to ask. The real quality elevators will be honored to work with you. The ones who say no were not the right person in the first place. But you'll never know if you don't ask.

The absolute best way to use this book is:

1- Set a five minute time every day to sit down with your elevator (mentor).

2- Read one section every day, talk about it and then stop. Do this every day until you finish the book.

3- Type (or write very neatly) each day's affirmation which appears on the bottom of the right page. Keep this in a safe place.

4- As you accumulate your personal affirmations every day, read them out loud to yourself every night just before you go to sleep. Each affirmation needs to be read for 21 days in a row (start over if you miss).

If you'll use this book exactly as I have outlined, incredible things will start happening in your life . . . guaranteed. Trust me for now, I'll explain why later.

Intro
for Parents (Guardians)

Get ready! By now, I hope you know the mission of this book. As a dad, I have agonized about how to stay close to my children as they pass through that critical part of growing up called adolescence. The world is a whole lot different now than it was when we were kids. It's scary! One thing I know for sure is that even though technology and the world change every day, there is one thing that stays the same . . . human nature. The successful principles of life and parenting remain constant. As long as we can determine these principles and blend them into our lives, we can rest in knowing that we have been great parents. Our children will ultimately choose their own direction but we can have a powerful part in how they choose. Sadly, most parents are clueless as to how to be a great parent. Bad parenting gets passed from generation to generation along with everything that goes with it . . . losing attitudes, addictions, divorce, etc.

For you, Mom and Dad, this book is part of the solution. Screening what your children watch and listen to, building trust, keeping them active, church involvement, quality food, exercise, consistent discipline, associating with good people, encouragement and you being a positive role model are all components of a comprehensive parenting program. My heart's desire is that you realize that great parenting is a continual growth process. Will this process guarantee that your child will have a perfect, problem-free life? No. But in the long run, they will return to the rock-solid foundation that you have given them. As your kids mature, they will love and appreciate you every day of their life as will your grand-children and your great grand-children.

In nature, once you stop growing . . . you begin to die. It's the same for parents and spouses. William James, the great behavioral scientist, said that if you can change a person's attitude, you can change their life. Let's change our attitudes about our children, our marriage, our selves . . . and get growing!

I don't care what your child has been like up until today. Each and every kid has a special gift. Unfortunately, most parents get caught up in all kinds of negative junk and our attitude toward our children is not what it should be. If you will commit just 5 minutes a day until this book is finished, I promise that great things will begin to happen for you and your child. Your kid did not ask to be born. At least equip them to be able to have a happy and successful life. This is an action book. What you put in, you get out. Love your child through this book.

If you're feeling totally inadequate, visit our website at www.powerworkshop.org. There's a booklist that will help you overcome any shortcomings you may have (real or imagined). Avoid the failure diseases – procrastination, excusitis, and detailitis. Let's get started.

1a
Dreaming Big Dreams

This is where it all begins. It doesn't matter where you have been but where you are going. I don't care where you live. I don't care who your mommy and daddy are (maybe you don't even have parents). I don't care what color your skin is. I don't care if you have been the worst student in the world (or the worst athlete, musician, or artist). I don't care if people have been calling you "loser" since the day you were born. I don't even care, if today, that you believe you are a "loser."

Every baby that is ever born is born for a reason. I'm convinced that each of us is born with a special gift . . . something important to give the world. Unfortunately, most people never realize that they are

1

special. Their gift is never opened. Their lives end up not being very happy or fulfilled. In order to have a great life, you need to figure out what makes you so special. You need to figure out what your your gift is. Get excited . . . this is your life we are talking about.

No matter where you are right now, there is a superstar inside you waiting to come out. I know that most of you reading this book don't believe me. If I am wrong, you'll be exactly the same after reading this book. But if I'm right (and I know I am), you will be on the road to success and happiness.

p.s.- *The road comes with bumps and potholes!*

affirmation #1a

I have a special gift inside me.

1b
What is a dream?

Good question. Well, we're not talking about the nightmare you may have had last night.

The dream we're talking about is the dream for your life . . . who you will become. If you've ever seen the Power Workshop, you'll remember grandma's hot water bottle. For those of you who have never seen a hot water bottle, let me explain. Made of very thick rubber, a hot water bottle is about 12 inches long and 7 inches wide. It has an opening at one end where people can fill it with hot water. Then they put it on whatever hurts. It's great for aches and pains.

I blow it up with lung power. When grandma's hot water bottle bursts, it symbolizes someone's head who has lost their dream. They become brain dead. Then it's only a matter of time before their body catches up and both (their dead dream and dead body) are buried together. Very sad.

What I'm talking about is developing a vision or purpose for your life. If you could be anything you wanted, what would it be? Don't let your vision be limited by what's around you or where you are right now. It might take 10 years, 20 years, or maybe even a lifetime to fulfill your purpose (destiny). Get excited because, whatever your dream is, it is worth going for it. Look around. There are so many people leading lives of "quiet desperation." People without dreams are sad and miserable. They usually always have an excuse why they've quit on life. Be careful not to let anyone steal your dream. It's very valuable. It's your life.

affirmation #1b

I am a person of vision.

1c
Dreambuilding 101

Let's do an exercise in order to let you see your dream more clearly. First, I need you to get comfortable and close your eyes. (Note: Do not clear your mind, I don't believe in empty heads.) Now you'll need your elevator to read the rest since your eyes should remain shut. With eyes closed, look up at what is really the back of your forehead and picture a blank chalkboard or wall mural. The picture that you begin to see is your life, your destiny. Many of you will find that there are distractions trying to keep you from seeing what's really on that chalkboard. There might be a little voice inside your head telling you that this is a stupid exercise. That's okay. On any road to success there are always obstacles and distractions.

   All right now, what do you think you might want to be? (Note to elevator: go slow and feel free

5

to add to the list) An artist, an actor, an astronaut, an athlete, a businessperson, a dancer, a doctor, a minister, a musician, an honest politician or lawyer, a scientist, a missionary? It might be something not on this list. It might be something so huge that you can't imagine yourself ever getting there. That's okay. Keep that picture. We'll talk about how to get from here to there later. For now, the most important thing is to see, to have vision. Open your eyes.

What if you didn't see anything? What if it's confusing and not clear? What if you can't focus? Does this mean that you're dream dead? Relax. Some people just need to be patient, pray, and work on gradually bringing their dream into focus. Like the lens on a pair of high-powered binoculars, just take some time everyday to bring your dream into clear view. You've begun the most important part of your journey. You've taken a huge first step.

affirmation #1c
I am excited about my dream. It gets clearer everyday.

1d
Why are we doing this?

Every once in a while, there'll be someone who is frustrated ask this question. Why? Why now? Because it's never too early to have a direction for your life. Most kids lose their way in life before they ever get started. Do you think that the "losers" in life are that way because they dared to dream big dreams? I don't think so. Probably, they were lazy and wandered around aimlessly until they got to where they were going . . . no-where.

Think about this. Every great person that you've ever heard of was once a kid. They had to go to school, make their beds, clean their rooms, do chores, deal with mom and dad, deal with brothers and sisters, do homework, reports, and science projects, walk the dog, go on family vacations, deal with family problems (like divorce and death), accept the weird changes that happen when you're becoming a teenager, hope for at least one good friend, deal with sickness, worry about what others thought of them, try to be good, and on and on and on. Just getting through a day can be rough. That's why the "Why" is so important. It gives you a reason to give your best effort and to have a positive attitude about life. Once you figure out "Why", the "how" is pretty basic. The "Why" is your dream, your vision, your purpose. The "Why" is so-o-o important for a happy and successful life.

affirmation #1d

I was born to be great, but it can only happen if I seek the wisdom of the ages.

2a
Grandma's Hot Water Bottle

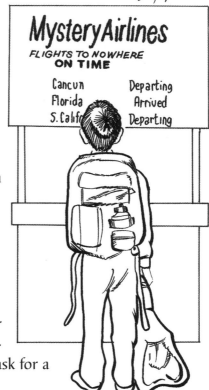

Grandma's Hot Water Bottle takes a lot of lung power to blow up. It's been said that it takes between 500 and 700 pounds of pressure for it to break. I don't know for sure but, believe me, it's not like a walk in the park.

Here are 5 things we can learn from Grandma's Hot Water Bottle:

1- Have a specific measurable goal. My goal in the show is to blow up the hot water bottle until it bursts. Setting goals is the best way to be sure of reaching your dreams.

Let's say that it's been a very cold, snowy winter. You decide that you've had enough of the freezing cold and that you're going to take a vacation. After packing your bags, you get a ride to the airport. You walk up to the person at the ticket counter and ask for a ticket. The ticket person asks "Where are you going?"

Not knowing the answer, you just stand there confused and say "Uh, I don't know. I never really thought about it."

    This may seem like an absurd story but there are millions of people out there who have no clue where they're going. They don't have a goal. They lack direction. Most people spend more time planning their vacations than they spend planning their lives. If you don't know where you are going, you're probably not going to like it when you get there.

affirmation #2a

    I set goals for my life.

2b
How did I reach my goal?

Grandma's Hot Water Bottle didn't just come out of the box and explode. I had to go for it one breath at a time. How do you eat an elephant? One bite at a time. Guess what? You won't be able to finish eating it in one meal. It's going to take a lot of meals. You're going to be eating leftovers for a long time. We're talking about achieving a long term goal. Is it worth it?

Well, if you believe that you have a special gift, if you believe that long term happiness and fulfillment are a good thing to shoot for, if you want to do something great with your life . . . then it is most definitely worth it.

Reaching goals is not something that just happens by itself. So many people see a huge elephant (goal) and become afraid. Do you know what they do? They quit before they ever start. They don't have the vision or belief that they can get from where they are to where their dreams and goals point them. If you'll refuse to be afraid and you set big, huge, humongous goals, life will really be special. Talk is cheap. It takes action to reach goals.

Here's an example that you can use. Let's say that you're 12 years old and someday you want to be a professional basketball player. Where would you have to be in 10 years in order to reach your goal? Well, you would probably be finishing a college basketball career at a major school where you distinguished yourself as a very special player.

Where, then, would you need to be in 5 years in order to reach your goal? Since you'll be 17 years old, you'll need to be in high school and playing at a very high level. Only the very best players are recruited to play at major schools.

If you're going to be ready to star on your high school team, where will you have to be by next year? You'll probably be in 8th grade. How good will you need to be at shooting, ballhandling, passing, defense, rebounding, etc.?

How much are you going to improve by next month? What will you need to do tomorrow? If you go through this process with everything you think you want to achieve, you will quickly discover if what you think you want is really a dream (real) or just a fantasy (not real). You will become passionate about your dreams and look forward to the challenges. Your fantasies will become a major pain and you'll look to avoid the work needed for success.

affirmation #2b

I write down my goals. I do some work toward achieving my goals everyday.

2c
Do you need a coach?

Back in 1992, a guy handed me a hot water bottle and asked me if I thought I could blow it up until it burst. I'd seen it done on television once so I took it up to my mouth and took two mighty puffs into it. It got to be about as big as a softball and I thought that the back pressure was going to blow a hole out of the back of my head. I had to let it go and the air came rushing out. After I caught my breath, I looked up and the guy was standing there laughing at me.

I said that it would be impossible for me to blow that thing up. He agreed. If I kept trying to do it the way I was, either I would fail or the back pressure would blow a whole in my lung (this really happened to someone and they died, don't try this one at home, boys and girls).

So what did I need to do if I wanted to successfully burst a hot water bottle? I needed someone to teach me the right way before I failed . . . or died trying. I needed a mentor. I talked to you in the intro about elevators. Even though I was 39 years old, I still had to learn the best (and safest) way to reach my goal. Go back and read the intro again. If you're willing to be humble and ask for help, you'll reach your goals a whole lot faster. You'll also have fewer scars, both physical and emotional.

Remember, when you're picking a mentor, to check the fruit on their tree. Are they in life where you want to be? Make sure that the person giving you advice is not making things up as they go along. Opinions are like noses . . . everybody has one. You need to discern what is really truth from what just sounds good.

When I was a kid, it seemed like the only people I took advice from were losers. Oh yeah, they seemed cool and they talked like they had it together but when I finally looked closer, their lives were a mess. Be careful, don't leave your life to chance. Mentors are people who have been there and come through successfully. If you've ever seen a war movie, you know what a mine field is and how dangerous it is. Your friends and old fools can't get you through without getting blown up, but a good mentor can. Choose wisely!

affirmation #2c

I seek quality mentors for my life. I have the strength to ask for help.

2d
When to quit.

Just about every time I blow up a hot water bottle, the pressure is so strong that I want to quit. It's never easy. If you set a goal that's easy for you to achieve, it probably was not a worthwhile goal. Worthwhile goals are difficult, frustrating, challenging . . . and usually you want to quit at some point. When you have to push yourself to new heights, you're on the right track.

The funny thing about the hot water bottle is that I never know when it's going to burst. I just know that if I refuse to give up, if I persist through the resistance, that

I will reach my goal and the hwb will explode. If I quit on the 19th breath, it may have exploded on the 20th. I'll never know, but the haunting question 'What if I hadn't quit?' will stay with me forever.

Just know that when you're trying to do something great with your life, there are going to be obstacles and hard times. It happens to all of us. Figure out a way to keep driving forward and laugh at the adversity. Know where you are going and trust that the right doors will open for you. Even if things look really bad and you can't imagine anything good coming of it, know that things never stay the same. In nature, things are either growing or dying. It's the same with your life. Keep growing and good things are going to happen. I really believe that. Do you? Keep the faith.

affirmation #2d
I know that nothing can stop me, I persist through resistance.

2e
T.E.A.M.

The last point I want to make about Grandma's Hot Water Bottle is about support and help. Accomplishing worthwhile goals is usually the result of a team effort. It's always ten times harder to burst the hwb alone at home than it is at a Power Workshop. Why? Is it just an adrenaline pump? I don't think so.

When I'm at a show, my wife is cheering for me, the music is cranking, the audience is yelling and screaming, and an energy begins to flow. One name for it is group synergy. Another is T.E.A.M. work. Together Everyone Achieves More. Sounds wonderful, but does it really work? Yes. Life is all about people pulling together to do something special. Sometimes people will be cheering for me, sometimes they'll be cheering for you.

How does something like this work in school? Let's say that you're pretty good in math. Someone sits across from you in class who is totally clueless when it comes to math. If you just sit there and take care of your own work, good is as far as you're going to get. If you want to be great, you need to help that kid across from you. I'm not talking about giving answers or cheating. You need to offer your help . . . after school, during lunch, e-mail, whenever you can work it out. Share some ideas or offer encouragement (we all have weaknesses). When you build someone else up, it lifts you to another level. The greatest and happiest people who have ever lived were the ones who lifted up and helped others. Dr. Schuller once said that the secret to happiness is to find a hurt and heal it. I believe it. So get out of the "what's in it for me?" mentality and a fantastic support team will emerge.

One hot water bottle, five strategies for getting from where you are to where you want to be. Set a goal, go for it one step at a time, get a mentor, be too tough to quit and become come part of a positive team.

affirmation #2e

I build up, help, comfort, and encourage others at every opportunity.

3a
The Wall of Negative

One of the highlights of a Power Workshop is when there is a huge stack of bricks and I break them with one blow from my arm. Everyone always asks, "Doesn't that really hurt?" The answer is "Yes!" But if it helps kids remember the message, then it's worth a little pain.

The stack of nine bricks symbolizes the type of negative wall that people usually build around themselves. If you have a negative wall built around yourself, achieving your dreams and goals may not be possible. Most people build walls around themselves and then they can't get out. We should be building bridges to other people. Think about that. So many gifts are wasted because of the walls people have built around themselves. If you're shy or afraid, if you try to be someone that you're not, if you don't like yourself, or if you're violent, then you've already started to build that wall of negative. We need to deal with the wall. Now.

affirmation #3a-
I am aware of the negative forces in my life. I face them.

3b
All great people know about the wall.

There's a basketball player named Mugsy Bogues. Imagine for a minute that you're in 5th grade and Mugsy is the new kid in your class. He's about the size of a 1st grader, yet he walks around school bouncing a basketball saying, "I'm going to be a pro basketball player someday. I'm gonna be a pro someday." All the other kids take one look at this little guy and laugh to themselves. Mugsy just ignores them.

Then about 6 years later, Mugsy is bouncing a basketball down the hallway at his high school saying, "I'm going to be a pro basketball player someday. I'm gonna be a pro someday." By now people are saying, "Hey Mugsy, don't you know that basketball players are 6 and 7 feet tall . . . you're only 5 foot?"

21

Mugsy just ignores them.

A few years later, Mugsy is in college and he's bouncing a basketball around the campus saying, "I'm going to be a pro basketball player someday. I'm gonna be a pro someday." At this point, people are laughing out loud that this full grown, five foot three inch little man actually believes that he can be a professional basketball player.

Well, the story ends with Mugsy Bogues being a star player in the NBA; he had become a pro. But this is not just a basketball story and I'm not saying that anyone who's short can do what Mugsy did. The important thing was Mugsy's vision. From the beginning, whenever Mugsy looked in the mirror he didn't see some little short guy. He saw what was on the inside, he saw his dream, his destiny. The reflection in the mirror is not the real you. The real you is on the inside, it's your heart and soul. Mugsy knew that the people who said he was too short didn't know the real truth. He had a vision. He went for it. He understood about the wall of negative.

affirmation #3b-
The real me is on the inside.

3c
Other great people who knew about the wall.

Maybe you just can't relate to a too-short basketball player. By now, I'm sure you've studied some history and know the name Abraham Lincoln. He was the greatest president in the history of the United States. The decisions he made, the principles he stood for, the way he led his life, the way he truly cared . . . the story of his life is really incredible. Yet, if you ever really study his life, you'll hear a story of a man who had more adversity, challenges, tragedies, and disappointments than anyone else I've ever heard of. He overcame them and became our greatest president. Abraham Lincoln knew how to break through the wall of negative.

23

Once there was a lady who, when she was a little baby, became unable to see or hear. The name of this special woman was Helen Keller. Can you imagine being blind and deaf for five minutes? How about for your whole life? It's difficult to imagine. Yet, this remarkable woman had a dream for her life and she refused to quit. She ended up reaching millions of people around the world in a positive way. Helen Keller knew that she had to break through the wall of negative in order to succeed.

affirmation #3c-

Life's not easy. Challenges make me stronger.

3d
The bricks have names.

Once I realized that a wall had been built around me, I was able to develop a plan of escape. Most people don't even realize that there's a wall built around them. They sense that something is not right in their life but they're unable to figure out what it is. It's the wall.

Now, my bricks had names. You may have a few bricks that are different than mine, but most people share a lot of the same bricks. The names of my nine bricks were envy, frustration, hate, guilt, revenge, insecurity, fear, laziness, and bad attitude.

Envy made me think that other kids had it better than me. They were smarter, better looking, had more friends and cooler parents, went on better vacations, had nicer clothes, etc., etc. . . .

25

Frustration had me thinking that so many things were difficult to do. Most things never came easy to me . . . schoolwork, sports, making friends, keeping my parents happy, etc.

Hate was something I learned when I was young. It was easier to hate someone or some group than to take the time to understand them.

Guilt was from all the bad things I'd done and all the opportunities to do good that I had missed. When I failed to use my gifts for something positive, I felt some heavy-duty guilt.

Revenge is very ugly. Every time I got back at someone who had hurt me, it seemed to make the whole situation worse. My mom was right when she said that two wrongs never make things right.

Insecurity sneaks up on you in a lot of different places. I needed to build confidence and belief in who I am. When you conquer insecurity, your strength will soar.

Fear paralyzes people. We're born with it. I'll tell you more about this one later.

Laziness almost destroyed my ambition. I used to try to save my energy. I confused energy with rest. When you're lazy, you waste time and time is the stuff that life is made of.

Bad attitude was the ugliest and hardest brick in my wall. In a lot of today's television shows and movies, many of the heroes are bad. It was the same when I was a kid and I used to practice being bad. You know, things like 'I'm tougher than you,' 'My dog barks louder than your dog,' 'I can spit farther than you can,' 'I can jump higher,' . . . well, you get the idea. I practiced being bad for a long time until one day I reached my goal. I was bad. The problem was that I wasn't happy. My attitude stunk.

There's an old saying that goes like this: "You're attitude in life will determine your altitude in life." This means that with a bad attitude your life will never get off the ground; a good attitude and you can soar with the eagles. This is one of those absolutes, it works all the time for everybody. If you want to be happy and successful, choose wisely.

We have just constructed a serious wall.

affirmation #3d-

I have identified the things that are holding me back. I know the enemy.

3e
It's breakthrough time.

Visualize this huge stack of bricks in front of you. The audience is pumped, the music is cranking, the countdown for the big break begins 10 . . .9 . . . 8 . . .7. . .6 . . .5 . . .4 . . .3 . . .2 . . .1. The arm comes down with tremendous force and the bricks seem to explode as they fly in different directions. Victory.

You're probably thinking that I'm some sort of karate guy who goes around smashing things. Not. In fact, a few years ago I was visiting a church and after the service a guy came up to me and asked if I could help him out. He was scheduled to do a show that night for a group of teenagers and he needed someone to help break some bricks. I thanked him for asking and told him that, basically, I was just an old basketball player.

29

In addition, I wasn't a karate guy and, although I'd lifted some weights, I wasn't particularly strong. He'd better find someone else to do his brick-breaking.

Well, he was insistent and my wife, Lin (who's a very supportive woman), said, "Go ahead and help the guy." The next thing I knew, I was driving down the Garden State Parkway with this guy from San Diego and he's telling me about the fine art of breaking bricks. We arrive at the show and there's a big room, packed full of people. There are two large stacks of bricks on the stage and I'm told that the one on the left is mine. Nine two-inch thick bricks, no practice. Can you picture this?

It was like being at a concert or a sports event. Everyone was pumped. The music was cranking, lights flashing and the crowd was loud. The show starts and I get on stage in front of my stack of bricks. Now, up until this point I was caught up in the excitement. It was great. They started the countdown. 10 . . .9 . . . Suddenly, all of that excitement just drained right out of me. I became filled with fear. This wasn't your ordinary, everyday fear. This was deep, down in your stomach, knees knockin', hands sweatin' when it's cold, FEAR.

I was afraid of three things. First, I was afraid that I was going to break my arm. Second, I was afraid that, once it broke, it was going to be very painful (and I don't like pain). And third, I was afraid that the bricks weren't going to break and everyone was going to be laughing as they took me to the local hospital. It sounds funny now, but it was quite serious at the time.

All of a sudden, right in the middle of the countdown, I remembered part of a speech that I had heard a few years before. The speaker said that faith and fear cannot live in the same body at the same time. I walked around for a week repeating, "Faith and fear cannot live in the same body at the same time. Faith and fear. . ." What was this guy talking about? It finally hit me. He meant that some things in life are all or nothing. It's like your best friend saying to you, "I'll always be your best friend . . . 99%." 99%? Wait a minute. How do you know when that 1% is going to sneak in? When will your best friend just leave you?

Either you're my best friend or not. That's it. No in betweens. No almost. Yes or no. All or nothing. It's the same with faith and fear. You choose. What's going to control your life? Look around and see how fear cripples the vast majority of people. Worry, anxiety, panic, doubt, misbelief, mistrust . . . fear vs. faith, belief, confidence, hope, trust. Which one will you allow to rule your life? Years ago, I read that we are born with two fears, fear of falling and fear of loud noises. All the rest of our fears are learned or imagined. It's definitely something you need to think about as you move ahead with your life.

So anyway, there I was staring at these bricks in a near panic. It was time to put up or shut up. Do or die. I chose total faith, prayed like never before, jumped up, and totally smashed that stack of bricks. They went flying in all directions. There was no one in the place more excited than me. It was wild.

The good news is that you don't have to smash a stack of bricks to break through the wall of negative in your life. The breakthrough actually happened before I even hit the bricks. The breakthrough came in my mind. The bricks were just a symbolic detail that forced me to face my fear. You may not have a pile of bricks like I did, but you will have something big that you have to face . . . and defeat. You may call it a defining moment where, how you respond, will set the course of your life. It will be your test. Know that it's coming. Enjoy it. Choose wisely.

affirmation #3e-

I make a move in faith to be courageous. I will crush the wall of negative in my life.

4a
The Red Dragon

Even though you break through the wall of negative, there's still one more thing you're going to need to deal with. It's called the little voice of self-doubt and negativity. It's that little voice that pops into your head at the worst possible time. It tells you things like you're too short, too tall, too fat, too skinny, too klutzy, too slow, too stupid, too late, too young, too old, or that you're the biggest loser ever born to the worst parents in the world.

Everyone has the little voice, even pro athletes. It always tries to sneak up on you at the worst possible time, like before (or during) a test, a big game, a play, or whenever you're not feeling your best. You need to recognize the voice for what it really is and defeat it. I never get in physical fights with other people, but I do fight the forces that try to steal peoples' dreams. Especially mine. I like to compare this voice to a big, red dragon.

affirmation #4a-

I recognize and fight the little voice of negative in my mind.

4b
Red Dragons?

Just imagine for a minute that you have a big, red dragon on your back. It's kind of hanging on your back. The big, old, red snout is over the top of your head and there's a big, old, red paw hanging over each of your shoulders. A long, fat, red tail is dragging out behind you. Got the picture? The red dragon is the little voice of self-doubt and negativity that is trying to wipe you out.

Now, let's say that, up until now, you haven't been very good in math. You decide (after reading this book) to do something extraordinary for your next math test. Your goal is to score

100% plus get the bonus question. The plan is to study like never before and, for once, to totally go for it.

All of a sudden, the big red dragon rears it's ugly head, reaches over, and bites you on the neck. Ouch! It's painful. The dragon reminds you that you've never scored 100% in your whole life. You decide to just go for an 85 in the test and then the dragon leaves you alone.

The next day after practice, you start dreaming about how much you really love to play basketball. You picture yourself doing something great. As the star player on your high school team, you lead your teammates to a state championship. After receiving many scholarship offers, you attend the best university in the country and your contributions lead to a national championship. During your junior year of college, you're invited to try out for the national team. After being picked, you travel around the world with the team for a whole summer. The following year, you are chosen to play on the United States Olympic Team and you win a gold medal.

And then, all of a sudden, the big, red dragon reaches over and bites you on the neck. Owww! It's painful. How can little, old you get from where you are to a gold medal? No way. Maybe you should just try out for the recreation team and see what happens. Once you stop dreaming big dreams, the dragon will leave you alone.

affirmation #4b-

I will not compromise. I will run to my dreams, not from them.

4c
Average

Any time that you're willing to be average, the red dragon will leave you alone. Any time that you want to do something great, the dragon will be all over you. What's the definition of average? The best of the worst and the worst of the best. Is that where you want to be? I don't think so.

Let me explain. If the dream for your life has nothing whatsoever to do with math, then is it okay to score an average grade? Since we all have different talents and abilities, sometimes an A is not attainable. But if you don't give your best effort in math, you may get lazy and miss an opportunity. I believe that most kids can get an A in math if they're willing to be patient and do some work. Is it worth it? Yes! Whatever work you are given, you should put out a good effort to get it done. The work that's related to your dream will be more enjoyable but might not be easy.

Get a solid understanding in all your school subjects. It's your foundation for building toward your dream.

When you start moving in the right direction, you'll develop a passion for knowledge. The red dragon, the little voice of self-doubt and negativity will be there at every turn. "It's too hard." "Watch tv, it's more fun." "If you don't hang with your friends, you'll miss something." "You're too tired." "It's not worth it."

affirmation 4c-

When it comes to my dream, I'm way above average.

4d
Getting the dragon off your back.

Even though I'm not a karate guy, my friend, Tommy White is a second degree black belt. He's taught me a few moves. One of them is excellent for getting dragons off your back.

See if you can follow these instructions. Stand up. Imagine the dragon on your back. Put your feet in the T position. Left foot facing forward, right foot back, perpendicular to the front foot. Stay balanced, knees bent slightly. Make a tight fist with both of your hands. Have your hands in front of your stomach. Elbows in. You're going to drive your right elbow into the heart of the dragon. It's a very powerful move. (Warning - Do not try this on little brothers or sisters or, for that matter, any other person.) In martial arts, one of the

39

important things to remember is the breathing. The ki-ai is that yell that gets the air going in the right direction. The louder the better. Maybe you should practice that first. Ready? 1-2-3! Haiii-Ah!!! Excellent. (I hope you're taking this part seriously, going through life with a dragon on your back is not much fun.) Okay, now let's put it all together. Check your feet, hands and elbows. Feel the dragon, hear it's voice, "You can't, you're a loser, it's too hard for you." Block out all distractions. Get loud. This is big. On 3. Drive that right elbow into the heart of the dragon. Ready? 1-2-3! Haiiiiii-Ah!!!!! Excellent. Good job. I know that you feel better already.

Yeah, this may be a funny illustration. Guess what? The important thing is that you recognize the dragon for what it is. It's going to keep coming at you. The voice will return. It will attack you at your weakest moments. So many people's lives are ruined by the red dragon. Most people don't even know what's destroying their lives. You do. Don't believe the lies that the dragon tells. You can defeat the enemy in your life.

affirmation #4d-

The red dragon has no power in my life. I've already won.

4e
OPDs

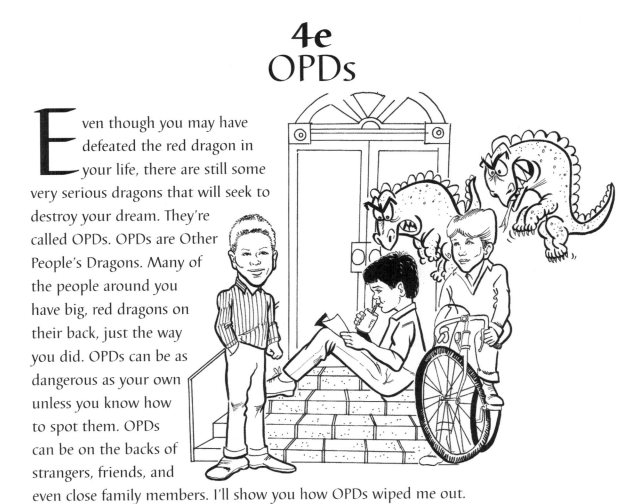

Even though you may have defeated the red dragon in your life, there are still some very serious dragons that will seek to destroy your dream. They're called OPDs. OPDs are Other People's Dragons. Many of the people around you have big, red dragons on their back, just the way you did. OPDs can be as dangerous as your own unless you know how to spot them. OPDs can be on the backs of strangers, friends, and even close family members. I'll show you how OPDs wiped me out.

When I was around 12 years old, my mom told me not to go down to the corner and hang out. She said that you become just like the people you hang with . . . losers with losers, winners with winners, fools with fools, wise people with wise people. My mom didn't think hangin' at the corner would be a good thing. I told her that I was a very good athlete, a boy scout, and almost a good student. She shouldn't worry, I'd never get like those guys at the corner. She still said, "No."

I believe that the first major mistake of my life was not obeying my mom. The corner seemed like a cool place to be. Once I got to know them, the guys became my friends. After a while, I began to walk like them, talk like them, dress like them, think like them . . . It was incredible how right my mom really was, but I didn't know it at the time. There's an old saying that "Pigs don't know how much pigs stink." This was certainly true for me.

Around this time I had a dream to be a great basketball player. Actually I thought that I was pretty good and that if I practiced, someday I would get a scholarship to a university to play ball. Every day that it wasn't pouring rain, I practiced. After a snowstorm, my friends and I would shovel off the courts and play basketball. We would have to leave our hats, coats, and gloves on until we warmed up. I was totally crazy about basketball and getting better all the time. After sitting the bench during 6th and 7th grade, I became a starter in the 8th grade and then led my team to the city championship in the 9th. It really seemed that my basketball career was taking off.

I shared my goal of getting a big time college scholarship with my friends. Guess what they said? They told me that college players are really tall and really strong and really fast. My friends reminded me that no one from our neighborhood had ever gotten a scholarship before . . . for anything. They didn't want me to get my feelings hurt if I didn't make it. My friends didn't want me to be disappointed. OPDs had their sights set on me.

My friends were unaware of the red dragons hanging on them. They were my friends and the little voice of self-doubt and negativity in them was speaking to me. My goals and dreams were under attack. OPDs are dreamstealers.

affirmation #4e-

I choose my friends carefully. I will not allow OPDs to steal my dream.

Russell and Lin Jones

4f
Spotting OPDs

Once you know that the enemy is out there, it's pretty easy to spot them. Dreamstealers usually use words like "can't" and "impossible" to the extreme. "You can't do that." "That's impossible." "You? No way." Sometimes, they'll just laugh at you. They may even try the same lies that your own dragon tried. "You're too short, too slow, too stupid, too late . . ."

Just watch out! Friends, strangers, family members . . . anyone who is not encouraging you to do something special, to stretch, to go for it, is a potential dreamstealer. Many people don't want you to succeed because they're lazy and your success will make them look bad. I've learned not to share my goals and dreams with just anyone.

If you ever visit the ocean and go crabbing, you'll notice that some people act just like crabs. If you catch one crab and put it in a bushel basket, it'll climb right up the side and escape. If you put it back in the basket, it'll climb up the side and escape again. No matter how many times you put it in the basket, it will climb out. But if you put 3 or 4 or 5 or more crabs in that same basket, as soon as one tries to get out, one will reach up with it's claw and grab on tight. Then another crab will grab the second one and hold on for dear life. Then another will grab on and then another. No crabs can escape. If they would all help each other, they could all escape to freedom. But they won't. They'll die in that basket before they let any one of them get out. Unfortunately, many friends and family can act just like those crabs. I feel sorry for people who act like crabs but I'm not going to let them keep me in their basket.

Dreamers build up other dreamers.

affirmation #4f-

I only trust my dreams to other dreamers.

5a
A Test of Strength

Let's change gears for a while and take a strength test. During one of my shows, I usually pick a big, strong guy to come up and I administer a two-part test. It's a lot of fun and you can try it at home. You'll need a heaping teaspoon of sugar, a cup of water and an empty cup. If you have any health problems where sugar can be fatal, do not try this. It takes two people so have your elevator available.

For the first part of the test, stand up, feet apart, knees bent slightly. Have your right arm straight out to the side with a tight fist (palm down) and keep your head facing forward (if you want to watch, do it in front of a mirror). Your helper should be standing behind you. To start, your helper should put both hands on top of your fist and apply steady, hard pressure downward for five seconds

(1 Mississippi, 2 Mississippi, 3 . . .). Try to hold up your arm with all your strength. It's important that the helper apply steady pressure and not rush it. Okay? Go! You and your partner should make a mental note of how hard they had to push.

Now for the second part of the test, put that teaspoon of sugar under your tongue. Do not swallow the sugar. Get in the same starting position as before. This time your helper should only use one or two fingers to push down. (Note to helper: There's no need to count this time, just apply pressure until the arm is at their side.) Ready? Go! What happened this time? Every time I do it, the person's arm always drops straight down to their side without much effort from me. One finger is all it takes. The first time it took two hands. I've done this with some really big guys and the result is always the same. Why?

Their are a few possible explanations but let me give you one that illustrates a powerful message. If I plant an apple seed, someday what will I get? Right, apples. If I plant an orange seed, someday what will I get? Oranges. If I plant a watermelon seed, someday what am I going to get? Watermelons. Whatever type seed I put in the ground, after some time, will give you the same type of fruit. So what has this got to do with the sugar? Well, everyone knows that too much sugar is bad for you. Sugar rots your teeth and causes all types of health problems down the road. Note that the results of eating too much sugar usually don't show up right away.

The reason that you could not hold up your arm is that a bad seed was planted under your tongue. The evil sugar seed was planted in your body and it dramatically weakened you. You were unable to hold up your arm. Usually it would take a long period of time before you would notice the weakness. But the high concentration of sugar under your tongue caused an almost immediate reaction. Seeds take time to bear fruit . . . good or bad. Give me some examples of junk food. If I continue to plant junk seed in my body, what kind of a body can I expect? Right . . . a junk body. It doesn't take a rocket scientist to figure out why so many people have weak, sick, out of shape bodies. Bad seed.

affirmation #5a-

Bad seed yields bad fruit. I choose carefully.

Russell and Lin Jones

5b
Your only body

We all get just one body per person for our whole life. Take a close look in the mirror. Head to toes, fingertip to fingertip. Is what you see in great shape? I'm not saying that we all need to look like a model or a super hero. Just healthy and strong. Your outward appearance indicates the type of seed that you're sowing in your body. The first time I really looked at myself in the mirror was on my 21st birthday. It was scary. Toothpick arms and legs, chicken breasted, bad posture, swollen stomach, no muscle tone, poor complexion, dry hair and scalp, weak, . . . what a mess. The bad seed had caught up. All the junk food was staring back at me. I decided to change.

affirmation #5b-

I take good care of the only body I will ever have.

5c
Three Other Seeds

There are three other seeds that I need to mention. Drugs, alcohol, and tobacco. By now, I'm sure you've learned all about this stuff and everyone has told you not to even try it. My perspective is a little different. Mike Deasy is a good friend of mine. He's the most recorded guitarist in history. I heard Mike talking one day and he said that drugs will do two things to you: "Drugs will kill you and drugs will . . . kill you!" I thought Mike had lost it when he said the same thing twice. I should have known better. My wise friend knew exactly what he was saying. Drugs (and alcohol, for that matter) kill in two ways.

The first way was how drugs killed a friend of Mike's who you may

53

have heard of. This guy was the greatest guitarist and rock star on the planet back in the late 1960's and early 1970's. I'm sure you've heard some of his music. His name was Jimi Hendrix. One day, at the top of his career, Hendrix came home from work and took a drug called cocaine. He also took a few pills and laid down. Friends found him later . . . dead. Hendrix had gagged on his own vomit and died. The most gifted rock star was gone in a heartbeat. It was like walking out between two parked cars and a big truck comes by . . . splat. I've had a lot of friends die this way. From when I was around 16 until I was 24, I attended 67 funerals. The deceased were kids I had grown up with. They died in different ways . . . car accidents, motorcycle accidents, overdoses, stabbings, shootings . . . The first way drugs will kill you is the fast way.

affirmation #5c-

My life is valuable. I'm here for a reason. I don't take unnecessary chances.

5d
The second way.

Then there's the kids who will say that what happened to Jimi Hendrix won't happen to them. Maybe they know some people who party who aren't dead. Maybe it's an older brother or sister. You may be reading this and you've already started having a few beers. Maybe you've smoked some dope. You're not dead . . . yet.

The second way that drugs will kill you is the slow way, the seed way. A good example of how this works is what I saw in high school. I played football, basketball, and baseball. Everyone was told that drugs and alcohol were especially bad for athletes. A lot of my teammates didn't believe it. They would party on the weekends and some even got high before and after games. I was confused. If drugs and alcohol were so bad, how come these guys could still play?

What I didn't realize was that a seed had been planted in these guys. It was bad seed and it was going to bear bad fruit. But it was going to take some time because some of my teammates were very talented. The bad seed eventually caught up with all of them. How? Well, it was like what happened to grandma's hot water bottle. They began to die on the inside. Their dream burst. They lost their motivation. They got lazy. The team wasn't as important as the party. Eventually, their only goal was to get high or drunk. They had become dream dead.

The second way that drugs, alcohol, and tobacco will kill you is very sneaky. The red dragon will tell you that drugs are ok and that everyone that's cool is doing them. That little voice will tell you that life is too hard and that alcohol will ease the pain. Someone will tell you that you can stop whenever you want. It's all one big LIE. Are you going to get sucked in?

There's a line in a movie where this girl wants to give up on her dream because she's been rejected by the "experts." She's been working for years and is so frustrated that she's ready to quit. Her confidence is shattered. Then this friend of hers takes her out for a serious talk. They're talking things over and finally he says, "Don't you understand? Once you lose your dream, you die."

Drugs kill dreams. Alcohol kills dreams. Tobacco just kills. My friend Mike is right. You choose.

affirmation #5d-

I don't need to smoke. I don't need to drink. I don't need drugs. Life gets me high.

5e
Good Seed

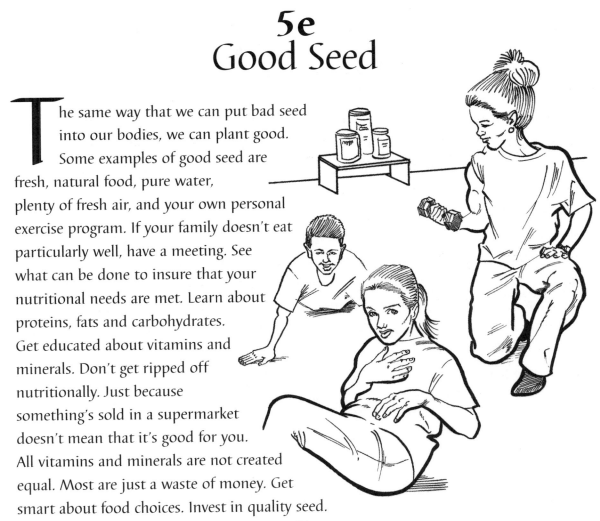

The same way that we can put bad seed into our bodies, we can plant good. Some examples of good seed are fresh, natural food, pure water, plenty of fresh air, and your own personal exercise program. If your family doesn't eat particularly well, have a meeting. See what can be done to insure that your nutritional needs are met. Learn about proteins, fats and carbohydrates. Get educated about vitamins and minerals. Don't get ripped off nutritionally. Just because something's sold in a supermarket doesn't mean that it's good for you. All vitamins and minerals are not created equal. Most are just a waste of money. Get smart about food choices. Invest in quality seed.

You also need to have your own personal exercise program. I'm not talking about team sports. You need an activity just for you. Something that you can do on a regular basis and not need anyone else to do it with. For me, it was lifting weights, pumping iron. Doing curls for the girls. I chose not to take steroids, so I didn't get as big and freaky as the 'roid boys. My strength was built by planting good seed in my body not by some quick fix. But I got real strong and it made me feel good on the inside as well as the outside. Natural athletes build their foundation on rock, the drugged athlete tries to build on a foundation of sand. If weight training sounds like something you might want to try, get someone to coach you who knows what they're doing and get started.

One of my sisters got into running, another got into swimming. Some of my friends like to bike and hike. Some are into martial arts. The point is that there are a whole lot of physical activities for you to choose from. Not everyone can be a great athlete, or even wants to be, but everyone needs to get physical. I don't care if you're an artist, a musician or a rocket scientist. You still need your body to be strong and healthy. Get started. Don't stop. Make fitness a lifetime habit, like brushing your teeth.

affirmation #5e-

I plant good seed in my body. I take care of what my body needs.

6a
Mind Seed.

The same way that you can plant seed in your body, you can plant it in your mind. You know that thing on top of your neck, behind your eyeballs, and in between your ears . . . your brain. Your brain is incredibly complex. Even though scientists will never be able to build something as special and unique as your brain, it works a lot like a computer. Instead of a keyboard, information is fed into your brain through your senses. Your eyes, ears, nose, tongue, and skin feed in all the data. The seed principle works here just like it does with your body.

What if you sat down at your computer in school and started typing in the words g-a-r-b-a-g-e space g-a-r-b-a-g-e space g-a-r-b-a-g-e? Then you hit the print button. What's going to come out on the piece of paper? Right. Garbage, garbage, garbage. Whatever you type into your computer is going to come out.

If you watch tv or go to the movies or listen to the radio, you know that there's a lot of bad stuff out there. Violence and immorality are common. There's a lot of negative stuff, bad attitudes. People tell ethnic and racial jokes. All of this is bad seed. Most people think that just because something's not physically touching them, that they're not affected. Wrong. Things that we see and hear affect us big time. Wise people understand GIGO. Garbage in, garbage out. If you keep allowing garbage into your mind, what's going to come out of your mouth? My Uncle Freddy used to say, "The top of my head is not a garbage can, don't dump here."

What I'm telling you is very important. Don't automatically trust the media. Be very careful. If you've seen the Power Workshop, you'll remember that I bend a 60 penny nail in half. My wife, Lin, shows the nail before and after. Her message is that some things appear to be straight and true when you first see them. Upon closer inspection, they're really bent and twisted. Use your mentors to help you discern the truth.

affirmation #6a-

Garbage is not allowed near my computer, my brain.

6b
Specific examples.

There are certain television shows that, on the surface, appear to be okay. Maybe they're comedies that make you laugh. They might be very popular. I was watching one of these shows and, after a while, it became clear that something wasn't right. The type of joking and teasing on this show was what I call put-down humor. You know the type of show I'm talking about. Put-downs, making fun of other people, ethnic or racial jokes, it was all there. So what? It's funny, it must be ok. Wrong.

When the humor is negative and nasty, it affects you in a bad way. How? The same way hanging with dreamstealers affects you. You become like the people you hang with. You become like the people you hang with on tv. You start telling the same type of jokes. Putting down and making fun of others becomes normal for you. If you're constantly putting down other people, you have a major problem. You don't like yourself.

By putting down others, you're trying to build yourself up. You think it's cool. Very wrong.

I'm ashamed to say that I was one of those kids who was always putting others down. I thought it made me better than other kids and my "cool" friends loved it. I had a bad mouth and a bad attitude. The problem was that, during those years, I really didn't like myself. I didn't understand the seed principle. It didn't matter that I was big and strong. Most kids were afraid to say anything back if I mocked them. The seed I was planting was bad and bad fruit was coming back to me. The scary part is that you never know when the bad fruit is going to come back. But it always does come back. It's a natural law.

The price you pay for putting someone else down, . . . for hating someone, . . . for prejudice, is that you make yourself less. You can't constantly be putting someone else down, or hating them, and still like yourself. In nature, things are either growing or dying. It's the same in your life. Are you building up or tearing down? Are you sowing a seed of life or destruction? What you give out, you will get back.

affirmation #6b-

I treat others like I want to be treated. I give out good, so I know I'm gonna get good back.

6c
What if you're picked on?

It usually happens to most of us at some time when we're growing up. Some get it worse than others. Sometimes it happens when we change schools or if we're short or fat or slow or if we dress differently or if our skin is a different color or if we're not hanging with the "in" group or if we say something dumb or do something klutzy or . . ., well you get the idea. It seems like it's the end of the world and that it will last forever. The good news is that it's not and it won't.

During the Power Workshop, I usually tell some stories of famous people who were picked on when they were kids. Danny DeVito was very, very short, Sylvester Stallone had a terrible speech impediment, etc.

Many people rise above the lies, the bad seed that was put on them as kids. The sad part is that there are millions of people out there who never overcame being picked on when they were kids. They believed the fools who were saying bad stuff about them. Being different is a good thing. How boring would it be if every flower was exactly the same? We need to get excited about who we are. The times of being picked on will pass. Don't waste your time worrying about it. Keep working toward your goals and dreams.

We all have weaknesses. From the most beautiful models to the good-looking superstar athletes to you and me. No one is perfect. Some people's weaknesses are more obvious than others. But we all have them. The thing that sets you apart is really the thing that makes you special and unique. If you're picked on, your reaction will determine your success or failure. Remember that in every adversity lies the seed for an equal or greater benefit . . . IF you look for it.

affirmation #6c-

Tough times never last but tough people do. No one's allowed to put me down.

6d
Good seed for the mind.

What can you do to pump yourself up? How can you energize yourself? One way is to keep in touch with other dreamers. Positive people will always build you up. Invest time hanging with people who are doing something special with their lives. They don't have to have the same dreams or gifts that you have. A couple of my best friends are world class musicians. I've never learned how to play any musical instruments. The only thing we have in common is that we're dreamers.

That's all we need. They encourage me and I encourage them. Hang with winners and you'll be lifted up. A rising tide raises all ships. Just make sure your boat is in the water.

Special books are good seed. They may be literary classics or what are called PMA books. PMA stands for positive mental attitude. Since your "attitude will determine your altitude" in life, this type book can be invaluable. Some of the best authors to look for are Dale Carnegie, Ben Sweetland, David Schwartz, Maxwell Maltz, Norman Vincent Peale, James Allen, Og Mandino, Cynthia Kersey and Zig Ziglar. These authors will help you get on and stay on the right track.

Music can be really good for you or really bad. I don't believe that the type of music you listen to is that important. You may like rock, classical, country, jazz, hip hop, rap, ska, gospel, oldies, newies or something else. However, the lyrics can wipe you out. All the violent, immoral, ugly stuff that we've been talking about is a big part of a lot of music. Avoid it like the plague. Music is very, very powerful. The messages get played over and over again in our heads. It becomes a part of you. To demonstrate this, my friend, Mike Deasy was playing guitar for a large audience. He played three notes from a commercial he had done 30 years ago. Everyone in the crowd who was alive back then remembered all the words to the commercial. Their minds acted just like computers and stored all that information. That really made me think about what our minds are exposed to everyday and the damage that can occur. In our house, we've been able to find all types of great music with positive, inspiring messages.

TV and movies can also provide some good seed if you're willing to check things out. There are enough great movies to keep you entertained for years. The list is long but some of my favorites are *Iron Will, Rocky, Cool Runnings, Rudy, Hoosiers* and *Chariots of Fire.* Hang out with winners on tv and in the movies. It'll keep you psyched.

Do not be upset with negative results in your life if you allow negative seed in your life!

affirmation #6d-
I choose to be a positive person. I sow good seed.

Russell and Lin Jones

7a
Paul

The most popular story that I tell at Power Workshops is about my friend, Paul. He was born many years ago with Bright's disease. Bright's disease is an acute kidney disease that kills most people. Obviously, if you don't have your kidneys, you're not going to live very long.

Paul was very sick as a kid. He missed a lot of school and spent many hours in the hospital. Because of his condition, Paul usually couldn't run and play with other kids. It was not a fun time.

When Paul reached high school, something miraculous happened. Between the prayers of his mom and some very good doctors, Paul had become healthy enough to play football for the first time. By 12th grade, he was a good enough player to get a college scholarship. Paul went away to college and played football for one year. But something wasn't right. He didn't feel good about school and came back home to talk it over with his parents.

It was around this time that Paul went over to visit one of his friends. Down in the basement of his friend's house, a few guys were lifting weights. Paul was around 19 years old at the time and had never really lifted before. He watched for a while and then walked over to a barbell that was lying on the floor. It weighed 200 pounds. He picked it up and put it across his shoulders. Then, Paul performed 20 full squats, all the way down and all the way up. His friends were watching and got really excited about the way Paul easily handled the heavy weight. There was something special about how he felt after the lift and, after that day, he was hooked. Persistently, Paul showed up at his friend's house almost every day . . . to lift.

Within a year and a half, Paul was hoisting heavier weights in his friend's basement than the Olympic champions were lifting. His friends encouraged him to go into competition. Heeding their advice, Paul began to prepare for his first major weightlifting contest. Four weeks before the meet, he was practicing a special lift called a belt squat. The weight was very heavy and, as Paul went to stand up, the muscles in his right thigh ripped. The pain was excruciating and he fell down on the platform. Paul had to be taken to the hospital where the doctors tried to repair his leg. Obviously, Paul couldn't compete in his first competition.

After a year of rehabilitating his leg, Paul was ready to enter another competition. It was held in Philadelphia and Paul was feeling stronger than ever. The first lift of the meet was called the press. In the press, there are two stands coming up from the floor to shoulder height. A barbell is placed across the stands with the weights loaded on both ends. The lifter steps up, grabs the bar and holds it across the front of the shoulders. After stepping back, the weight is pressed directly overhead to full arms length. When the judges light the green light, it's a good lift and you can drop the weight.

Since Paul had been waiting so long for this day to arrive, he decided to really get the crowd's attention in a hurry. He had the barbell loaded with more weight than the national record. The crowd was buzzing since no one had really ever heard of Paul before. Here's a newcomer going for the national record on his first attempt. Who is this guy?

Out from behind the stage appeared my friend, Paul Anderson. The audience was stunned as my 5'9", 340 pound friend approached the bar. He was huge. All natural, no drugs. He was such a gifted athlete that, even at that incredible size, he could dunk a basketball. Paul stepped up to the bar and took a tight grip. He stepped back. Just as he went to press it overhead, his left wrist snapped. The barbell went crashing to the floor. His wrist was broken. For Paul, the competition was over. Not a good day.

When the doctor put the cast on,

Paul pushed a big hook inside. He figured that he could hook the weights while his wrist healed. Paul didn't want to miss a workout. I know this sounds a little crazy but Paul had a big dream and he wouldn't allow himself to be defeated. Non-dreamers couldn't understand why Paul would continue to push himself. Non-dreamers just don't get it. Obstacles are there to test you. Climb over, go around, tunnel under . . . do whatever it takes to get past mountains in your life. If that doesn't work, Dr. Schuller says to stay where you are and turn your mountain into a gold mine. Just don't quit.

By the end of that year, Paul's wrist was healed and his leg was feeling stronger than ever. He decided to enter another competition. As the day for the meet got closer, some of Paul's friends, who were home from college, came to visit. They saw that Paul had been working out for months without taking any real time off. His friends convinced him to come out with them on Saturday night. They were going to the county fair. After Paul climbed into the back seat, they took off looking for a good time. It had been raining that night and the roads were wet. They were stuck behind a slow moving car and Paul's friend, who was driving, decided to pass. As he pulled out to go around the vehicle in front of him, he lost control on the slick road. The car slid off the road, went into a ditch, and hit a tree. Everyone in the car was ok . . . except Paul. The car had struck the tree exactly where Paul was sitting in the back seat. Paul's hip and ribs were broken in the accident.

Sometimes when I tell this story, it seems unreal that so much bad stuff could happen to one person. But it's a true story. Obviously, Paul could not compete again. Three times he had attempted to do something great and three times he had been

wiped out. At this point, a lot of people were thinking Paul should get a desk job. Take it easy. Slow down. Maybe the injuries were a bad omen. But Paul wouldn't listen, he was on a mission that most people couldn't understand. By the following year, his hip and ribs had healed, his leg and wrist were strong and Paul was ready. It was 1955 and Paul Anderson won the World Championship in Munich, Germany. Finally, all the hard work, all the time at the doctors, all the doubt, and all the pain had paid off. Paul Anderson, World Champion! Yet, there was still some unfinished business.

In 1956, the Olympics were being held in Melbourne, Australia. Paul wanted to finish his amateur career with a gold medal. The entire U.S. Olympic Team arrived in Melbourne two weeks before the start of the games. All the best athletes in the world were there getting ready for the biggest competition of their lives. Paul was there for two days and he got a fever . . . 104 degrees. There were still 12 days left and everyone figured that he just had a virus. Everyone was wrong. Even the doctors had failed to diagnose an infection that was causing the high fever. The 104 degree fever lasted the whole 12 days leading up to the competition. Paul couldn't eat. He couldn't workout. He could hardly get out of bed. While all the other athletes were getting in the best shape of their lives, Paul was losing 40 pounds of muscle. Not a good thing.

It looked as if Paul was going to have to go home without even getting a chance to lift. But Paul had different plans. He entered the competition anyway. On the first two lifts, Paul managed just enough points to qualify for the finals. The last lift of the night was called the clean and jerk. If you've never seen it performed, you might want to stand up and try it.

On this lift, the barbell is on the floor. You grab the bar a little wider than shoulder width, palms down. Your shins should be against the bar, head up, back flat. Now, in one motion, pull the weight from the floor as you begin to rise up. Keep the bar close to your body and pull it up to your face. Now flip your wrists and cradle the weight at the top of your chest, the base of your neck. That's the clean part. It needs to be a very explosive movement. Now that the bar is up by your throat, you need to raise it to arm's length overhead. This phase is called the jerk. As you dip your body down into either a squat or a front split, the bar is quickly rammed up to arm's length overhead. To finish, raise up out of the squat or split and hold the weight overhead. When the judges have determined that you have the bar under control and that it's a good lift, the green light will light and you can drop the weight. Got it? This particular lift not only requires strength but also a high degree of speed and coordination. It's extremely difficult to perform correctly and takes years of practice to perfect. Don't expect to see this lift at your local gym or weight room. The muscleheads and guys working their beach muscles usually stay away.

Since Paul was so far behind in points, in order to win the gold medal, he would have to set a new Olympic record. To win, he would have to clean and jerk 414 1/2 pounds. If he breaks the Olympic record and wins the gold medal, his teammates will also have won the team medal. Paul approached the bar for his first attempt. He cleaned it up to his chest . . . and dropped it.

Well, you get three tries and Paul went behind the curtain to rest. While he was there, the red dragon was all over him. The red dragon told him things like "You'll never make this lift, you're too sick. You're too weak, you'll have to come back in four years. It's impossible." Paul was desperate but he told himself that he hadn't come to Melbourne for second place. He had come for the gold. Can you imagine being in a sick bed for twelve days with a 104 degree fever and someone calls on you to set a new Olympic record? Major pressure. The red dragon was very real.

Paul came out for his second attempt. All his teammates were shouting words of encouragement. He grabbed the bar, pulled the 414 1/2 pounds up to his chest and . . . dropped it. Paul was down to his last chance and he again went behind the curtain. Things did not look good. Fear, doubt, frustration, anger, confusion, the infection . . . they took turns attacking Paul. Should he just quit and go home? Should he wait another four years to achieve his goal? A few years earlier, the famous English statesman, Winston Churchill had made a speech that was only four words. England was in a war and was facing an impossible situation. Here's the speech. "Never, never give up!" That's all Churchill said and he walked off the stage. Thoughts like that were rising up from deep inside Paul Anderson.

For the third and final attempt at the new record and the gold medal, the crowd was beyond tense. The anticipation had caused a highly charged atmosphere. The guys on the U.S. team were all standing and, more than cheering, they were begging for a victory. They knew Paul's condition and felt helpless as they could only hope for the best. Could the reigning world champion come from behind to win? Could he overcome the 12 days in bed with a 104 degree fever and the loss of 40 pounds of muscle? Would the infection cause permanent damage if he pushed his body past it's normal limits? Was it worth the price?

As he reminded himself that second place was not an option, Paul reached down for the bar. He set himself and pulled the bar with all his might. The heavy weight was resting uncomfortably across the top of his chest. It felt immovable. This was the same place he had gotten the bar on his first two attempts. He had failed both times to move the 414 1/2 pounds an inch further. For what seemed like forever, the bar laid across Paul's chest. Usually, it's only a quick pause and the lifter jerks the weight overhead but Paul was fighting to just control it. . . . 5 seconds, 8 seconds, 12 seconds . . . it seemed as if everyone in the audience was holding their breath.

Then at that moment of truth, at that moment of desperation, Paul did something he had never really done before. He prayed. Here's how Paul described the moment: "I became aware and told God that He had given me everything and I had returned nothing. I want to be part of Your kingdom, and from here on out, I'm making a real commitment. I'm not trying to make a deal God but I really must have Your help to get this weight overhead." He pushed with everything he had and the weight rose slowly overhead, the green light came on and Paul Anderson had won the gold medal. That was in 1956 and no American weightlifter has won it since.

The following year, Paul wanted to establish himself as the strongest man that had ever lived. A heavy-duty wooden table was constructed and weights were loaded on top of it. The combined weight of the table and the weights was 6,270 pounds. That's about the weight of two automobiles. Paul got under the table and lifted it off the floor. As he lowered the weight back to the floor, Paul had broken the Guiness world record by almost 2,000 pounds. In this unbelievable backlift,

Paul Anderson had raised more weight than anyone in history. Combined with his other accomplishments, Paul was truly the strongest man who ever lived.

affirmation #7a-

I overcome negative situations and feelings to reach my goals.

7b
What can we learn from Paul's experience?

Even though we're not all world champion weightlifters, there are a number of valuable lessons we can learn from Paul's experience. In many police academies across the country, there is a quote on the wall that says "the more you sweat in the gym, the less you bleed on the street." The first time I heard this, my oldest son was preparing to become a police officer. As a parent, the image of your child bleeding on the street is not something you want to be thinking about. Most things that we do carry a certain degree of risk, but the dangers

79

in police work are 'in your face.' The message from the quote is clear. If you sweat here at the academy, if you work hard, if you learn as much as you can, then you greatly reduce the chance of getting hurt. Intense preparation yields sharper reactions in life-threatening situations.

In sports, the players who prepare the most are the ones who come the closest to reaching their potential. The more you sweat in the off season working out by yourself, the harder you work in practice, the better you'll be in the game. Especially near the end of the game, when everyone's tired, the best prepared athlete will have a reserve strength to call on. It's just like money in the bank. If you have a plan to save money when you're 12, then you'll have enough to buy a car when you're 17. But if you don't start to make your deposits now, you'll wake up the day after you take your driver's test with $0 in the bank. When I was a kid in Boy Scouts, the leaders always had us repeat the motto about a million times. The motto was "be prepared." You don't have to be old to do something great. You just need to be ready. Opportunities are all around us but we usually miss them because we're not ready.

affirmation #7b-

The more I prepare, the more opportunities will come my way.

7c
Another way to sweat.

The way that Paul Anderson spent the years before the Olympics had a lot to do with his gold medal performance. His preparation included studying nutrition and eating right, studying the human body and lifting right, studying psychology and thinking right, as well as competing in order to gain experience and wisdom. It all paid off when, even though Paul was very sick, he was able to make a major withdrawal from his savings. If he hadn't invested in his weightlifting career, his account would have been empty.

Well, the same way that you can invest your money or prepare your body, you can prepare your mind. The more you sweat in the books, the smarter you'll be on the street. Statistically, 80% of all high school honor students cheat at some point in order to get better grades. Many kids feel pressure to do good in school. They figure that it's okay to cheat since the bottom line is getting good grades. Dumb, very dumb.

School is not about grades. School is about knowledge. If you can develop a love of learning, the good grades will follow automatically. If you're just trying to get through school, you're wasting your time . . . and your life. When you're applying for a job or in your own business, no one is going to care what grade you got in 8th grade math. They will care about what you know. If you cheat, everyone will know that you have a major deficiency. Understanding the concepts is very important. Please don't tell me that, based on your dream, you're never going to need math for the rest of your life. Another lie from the red dragon. The stuff you learn in school is part of your foundation. In a house, the foundation is what the builders construct first. It's the base that supports everything else. Without a strong foundation, the whole house is weak. If a big storm comes, a house with a weak foundation will crumble and collapse.

Cheating and not giving a good effort in all your school subjects will give you a weak foundation. When you go for a job or start your own business, no one will care what your grades in school were. People will want to know how much knowledge you have. Invest now.

affirmation #7c-

The more I sweat in the books, the smarter I'll be on the street.

7d
Competition

Another lesson we can learn from Paul Anderson is about competition. Paul would want you to know that, on the road to success, there are no shortcuts. You're going to have to pay the price. Not only will you have to compete against others with the same goals and dreams as you, you'll have to compete against yourself. Competition is a good thing. It will make you better and prepare you for the next level. Nobody ever said it was going to be easy. There are no shortcuts. The reason you can be successful is that most people are looking for shortcuts and get upset when things are not as easy as they thought it would be. Then they quit. You won't have much competition if you refuse to quit. In

83

every adversity lie the seed of an equal or greater benefit (if you look for it). Take some time to really understand the last sentence.

Paul Anderson was 'too tough to quit.' Everywhere you look at a Power Workshop, you'll see 'too tough to quit.' It's on our banner. It's on our pledge cards. It's even on our shirts. The tough I'm talking about is not some dumb musclehead thing. It's not about some big, ugly, macho dude walking down the middle of the street trying to scare and intimidate you. That's not tough, that's just ugly. I feel sorry for people who need to bully others, whether it's mental, physical or emotional. Their lives are miserable.

The really tough people are the ones who are 'too tough to quit' on their dreams. If a goal is missed, they reset, then re-commit, and go for it. Paul had every excuse he needed to give up and try again in four years. In the natural, there was no way he could win. Logical people knew that it was impossible for anyone as sick as Paul to perform at his best. The critics thought that Paul was crazy to even enter the competition. But the experts couldn't see what was inside Paul Anderson. They couldn't see his heart and his warrior spirit. They couldn't see his will to win. They couldn't see that he refused to give up. And when Paul added that small measure of faith, he was unstoppable.

affirmation #7d-

In every adversity lies the seed of an equal or greater benefit (if I look for it). I'm too tough to quit.

7e
Nail driving 101.

As you can probably tell by now, Paul Anderson is one of my all time heroes. A couple of years ago, I needed some new strength feats. Paul and his wife, Glenda, lived in Georgia where they run the Paul Anderson Youth Home. Since the 1960's, they have been taking in boys who were in big trouble with the law. Paul and Glenda would fill many roles for these young men. They trained the boys to lead productive lives and acted as their parents, teachers, and mentors. It's a major operation and the Anderson's have a very high success rate.

When I phoned Paul, I had no idea how sick he

really was. His kidney problems had returned as he had gotten older. When he was in his 40's, Paul had one of his kidneys removed and then the other a few years later. His sister had donated one of hers so that Paul could continue his extraordinary work at the youth home. Through all of his physical trials, he never stopped helping those in need.

I asked him if there was anything he could teach me that would help make our messages more powerful. One of the feats Paul performed during his career was nail driving. He would take a 20 penny nail and hold it in the palm of his hand with a rag. Then, with one mighty swipe, he would drive it through a thick piece of wood. It was incredible to see. No hammer. Paul Anderson taught me how to do it . . . over the telephone. Six months later, he went home to be with the Lord. Nail driving, and the message that goes with it, has become one of the cornerstones of the Power Workshop.

After I drive the nail through, two people are usually invited to try and pull it out. Since the nail goes through with one punch, the challenge is for someone to pull it out with one pull. A monetary prize is offered as a reward for getting the nail out. If the board doesn't split on impact, no one ever pulls the nail out. Of course, if you used a hammer or maybe if you bent the nail back and forth for a while, it would come out. But the deal is that, if it goes in with one hit, it has to come out the same way. How come no one ever pulls it straight out? Because it's a whole lot easier to do something, than it is to undo it. It's a whole lot easier to do something right the first time, than it is to try to undo it later on. Prevention is a whole lot easier than trying to find a cure later.

So when you have to make choices about sex, drugs, and alcohol, remember the nail. Some things in life can never be undone. Do the right thing the first time and you won't have to worry later. That's why knowledge and wisdom are so important.

affirmation #7e-

I always choose to do the right thing. My life is at stake.

Russell and Lin Jones

8a
The Pledge.

When you look out at the ocean, many times you'll see huge ships. Some of these monster boats carry thousands and thousands of pounds of cargo. Sometimes its hard to imagine how they're able to keep from sinking. Yet, the thing that controls the direction of the ship, the thing that controls where the huge boat will end up is this little piece hanging off the back. It's called the rudder. The rudder controls whether the ship goes straight, or left, or right, or does a U-ey. It's incredible how much power that little rudder really has.

The rudder in your life is a little thing inside your mouth. It's called your tongue. Ultimately, where you end up in life is a result of how you speak. I know it sounds crazy but it's true. Just listen. I'm not talking about accents or even proper English. I'm talking about the substance of your words. People, who are losing in life, most definitely speak the part. People, who are winning in life, most definitely speak the part. As I began to understand how powerful words are, it really scared me.

By the age of 29, my life had been one major mess after another. Some business people showed me how my mouth was the reason for my failures. They gave me books of wisdom to help prove their point. They talked about being 'hung by my tongue" and 'snared by the words of my mouth.' What they said made me shut-up for about two weeks. If what they were saying was true, I needed to change. The only way to know if they were right was to try it. I did. It works for everyone. It even worked for me.

affirmation #8a-
The way I speak will control the direction of my life.

8b
Negative vs. Positive

From time to time, you will hear people described as either negative or positive. Most people don't really understand what that really means. For most of us, it's easy to identify the really negative people in the world. They always see the worst side of things and they usually expect the worst to happen. They're called pessimists and are usually very skeptical of anything good that's going on. If it's a beautiful, sunny day they're expecting a terrible storm to come at any moment. Actually, when a storm comes or something bad happens, they feel good because they were right.

But it wasn't easy for me to spot negative people. Again, there's that old saying that "pigs don't know that pigs stink." For pigs, smelling as bad as they do is just normal. When you're a pig, the rest of the pigs don't care how

you smell. They're all in it together. Well, that's how I was . . . just like the pigs. My friends, the people I was hanging with were so negative that I thought it was normal. I was so negative that positive, up-beat people seemed very strange to me. I couldn't relate to dreamers because my dream was almost dead. Dream-dead, down and out, negative people look for people just like them. They all hang together while whining and complaining and blaming away their lives. But in one miraculous moment, I changed the direction of my life. While I was a pig, I didn't even know that I could change. My life had been so empty, so desperate, so pathetic. Then I found out that I could change . . . and I did. If I can do it, you can do it, too. I believe that.

affirmation #8b-
I control the direction of my life.

8c
Candle light.

You may not be a really negative person. But maybe you're half negative or even maybe just a quarter negative. You have to be real careful because negative is a very powerful force. When your attitude slips even just a little, it can cause a landslide of discouragement. Sometimes a negative attitude will just set you back a little and then you can get right back on the positive track. However, sometimes a negative attitude can send you into a tailspin that could take years to get out of.

Okay, it's time to get the smallest candle you can find and some matches. Do this experiment at night or in a room without windows. Have all the lights in the room on. One at a time, turn off all the lights in the room. Just before you shut the last light, get the match ready. Make sure that no light is sneaking in under the doors. You should be in total darkness. This is what the negative world is all about. How can you go for your dreams when you're in total darkness? How can you

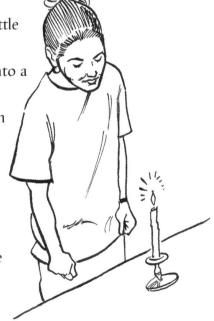

have 'vision' when there's nothing to see? No light, no color, nothing. Believe it or not, most people's lives are like this. No dream, just darkness. People's lives get swallowed up by the negative forces in life. After you shut the last light, take your time and look around.

Now, light the tiny candle. What do you notice? Is your attention drawn to or away from the candle? Leave the candle lit and try to make the room darker. All the darkness in the world cannot diminish the light of your one little candle. All the world's attention will be drawn to that light, no matter how small it is. The darkness is the negative side of life, the light is the positive. Can you understand why you need to be a positive force? This old world needs light. Joy and happiness are in the light. The only one who can totally extinguish your candle is . . . you.

affirmation #8c-
My candle burns brightly. No one can extinguish my light.

8d
Computer re-programming.

I hope that you're ready to take the necessary steps to become a positive person. It doesn't just happen. Since I was such a negative, skeptical person, it was important for me to understand the process. I needed to know how to control my rudder. So, it was a big step.

Remember when I compared your brain to the greatest computer ever made? Here's how you can program your brain for positive. During the Power Workshop, I challenge everyone to take the 'pledge.' The 'pledge' is a series of positive affirmations. I challenge everyone to recite the 'pledge' for 21 days in a row. It takes 21 days to establish a habit and good habits establish character. It has to be said out loud. Even though everything that you see, hear, and feel goes right into your computer, the most powerful thing that will influence you are your own words. The tv, movies, music lyrics, and other people around you can have a profound affect on who you become. But remember, what you say to and about yourself is of utmost importance. I don't care if you say the 'pledge' under your bed, in the closet, or in the bathroom. If you'll do it, I guarantee great things will begin to happen in your life.

The absolute best time to do it is just before you go to sleep at night. Why? Well the easiest way to understand is to know that you have a conscious and a sub-conscious mind. Right now, as you are reading this, you are using your conscious mind. It's the conscious mind that you use all day long. But when you go to sleep, your conscious mind shuts down. It goes to sleep, too. However, your sub-conscious mind is on duty 24 hours a day, everyday. It never sleeps. Everything you have ever seen or heard is being stored somewhere in your sub-conscious mind. It's like a huge sponge, it sucks up everything. Your sub-conscious mind doesn't care if the information coming in is right or wrong, true or false. It just keeps taking it in. That's why it's so important to limit the garbage intake as much as possible. Once it gets in your head, it stays . . . for life. Keep diluting all the negative junk that's already in your sub-conscious with all the good stuff you can find. Speak to yourself about how you want things to be, not how they are.

The reason that you should speak your positive affirmations just before sleep is important. The last thing to go into your mind before sleep is what your sub-conscious will work on all night long. This is a powerful tool that most people are not even aware of. You are.

The only way you'll know if this whole process really works is to do it. We hand out tens of thousands of 'pledge' cards every year and probably only one kid out of 500 is able to do it. The kids that do it usually call and share the excitement with us. What happens to the other 499? I used to think that it was because they were lazy but it only takes a few minutes a day. Probably the real reason is that they don't believe. It only takes the smallest amount of belief to say a two-minute pledge every day. It's not like I'm asking them to try something dangerous or really hard. If there was a chance to radically improve your life and it didn't take a lot of time or effort, why wouldn't you at least try?

Another possible reason why so many fail to do it is because no one is there to remind them. Kid's get to a point where they don't think for themselves. If no one is there to say 'do this' or 'do that,' kids just veg out. A lot of kids think that their teachers or their parents will always be there to push them. Not. We all need to develop self-discipline. We have to initiate the action to make our lives great. Set time aside for the important things like reading, exercise, helping others and . . . re-programming your computer, your brain.

affirmation #8d-

I have self-discipline. I make sure that the important things in my life get done.

Russell and Lin Jones

8e
Do it.

Where can you get your own 'pledge'? Well, you can copy all the affirmations in this book and use them. I suggest that you start the 'pledge' and do it for 21 days straight just before bed. Start over if you miss a day. By this time you should have a very powerful habit developed. Get with your 'elevator' and write your own personal affirmations. Base them on the areas of your life that need improvement. Repeat your own 'pledge' for 21 days and then write another by adding or subtracting new affirmations and old ones. Keep up the process to maintain a high level of personal strength and growth. If you say good stuff, talking to yourself is really valuable.

Someone always asks the question, "What if I memorize my pledge, do I still have to do it for 21 days?" The answer is "Yes!" The reason is this. Let's say that you want to grow huge arm muscles. You want to have the biggest guns possible. Since you don't know how to do it, you come to me for advice. I start out by telling you that, if you'll follow my program exactly, your arms will grow bigger than mine. You say, "Cool." After you get out your notebook, I tell you about all the exercises that you'll need to do. I tell how many sets and reps to do as well as how often to workout. Then, I give information about the types of food to eat and how much you'll need everyday. The right vitamins, minerals and other supplements are very important. Without adequate rest between workouts, your performance will suffer and you won't get good results. The right type of stretching is important for avoiding injury. Now you have all the information you need to have your arms grow to super human proportions. Finally, you take your notebook with all this valuable information and you put it in your desk . . . and you leave it there. Will your arms grow to their full potential? Will they become humongous? Of course not. Just because you know how to build your arms doesn't mean that they'll grow. You have to take action. Knowledge about arm growing is not enough. You have to actually get in there and do the work. If you workout once or twice, will your arms grow? Nope, they'll just get sore. To get the results you want, you must commit to doing the program over a long period of time.

Well, the 'pledge' works the same way. It's an exercise. It must be repeated over and over again, if you want to get results. The exercise is for the positive words to come out of your mouth, go into your ears, and sink deep into your computer, your brain. If you only do it for a few days, or when you feel like it, it won't work.

affirmation #8e-

I pledge to take action. Great habits yield great results.

Russell and Lin Jones

8f
Make your whole life a pledge.

...*I CAN'T DO THAT! ...IT'S TOO HARD!*

One final message for this section. Remember when we talked about how to recognize dreamstealers in your life? They use words like "can't" and "impossible" all the time. Their goal is to discourage you from doing something great with your life.

When you allow your rudder to speak words like that about you, it can be devastating in your life. Make sure that you only say positive, uplifting stuff about yourself. Don't forget that your sub-conscious mind takes in whatever you tell it. Speak only good stuff about yourself. Speak the new you into existence.

There's a girl on my basketball team who we call Big D. She's our center and also an excellent student. Big D is also a very nice person. My goal as her coach is to make her the best player possible. All my players have strengths and weaknesses in their game just like Big D. The problem is that I can see how good a player Big D can be, but she only sees how she is now. Someone close to Big D once told me that she would never be a good basketball player because she was too slow on her feet and couldn't jump high. I disagreed because I saw her strengths and believed that she could radically improve on her weaknesses.

She's an excellent rebounder and passer. Big D is very unselfish and a team player. The area of her game that she can really improve is her offense, particularly inside. I've worked with her to develop a powerful inside game where she can shoot a variety of shots with either hand. In practice against me, she does a great job and the other coaches agree that she has tremendous potential. Here's the problem. Big D doesn't believe me. During a game, she goes back to her same old habits and gets her same old results. It's frustrating to me and her but she just doesn't have the confidence . . . yet. Years of bad habits have to be torn down if Big D is going to reach her full potential. Still, the biggest obstacle she has to overcome is the way she speaks about herself. Her rudder is directing her to failure. When a player says things like "I can't do that," "I'm not good at it," "It's too hard," or "I hate practicing this," all their potential is being buried. Big D doesn't realize how she's undermining her own confidence by the way she speaks about herself. She's re-enforcing negative in her life. By saying things like "I'm getting better everyday," "If someone else can do it, so can I," "Challenges make me stronger," "I know that nothing can stop me, I persist through resistance," Big D would be on the way to becoming a great all around player. I hope she believes me someday . . . soon.

affirmation #8f-

I only speak good things about me . . . all the time.

9a
The Wrap.

Where I live, there are a lot of trees. Every year in the fall, there are a ton of acorns on the ground. Now an acorn can become one of two different things. An acorn can either become squirrel food or grow into a mighty oak tree. It's the same with your life. The squirrels are going to try to get your acorn. Some squirrel might try to give you something to smoke, or some alcohol to drink, or something to snort up your nose, or shoot in your arm. Or maybe some squirrel will just walk right up to you and say, "Yo, you're a loser!" And then you say, "Oh, thank you very much, Mr. Squirrel." I'm not talking about the furry little creatures that run up and down trees. I'm talking about the people in life who are trying to steal or destroy your dream. Just like the crabs, there are a lot of nasty people out there disguised as cute little squirrels. They're very dangerous.

Now let's say that you tell the squirrels, "Get away from me and my acorn. Stay out of my life!" You make the right choices in life. You hang with the right people. You get plenty of sunlight and the right amount of water. Your acorn grows to be a mighty oak tree. Cool.

affirmation #9a-

My life and my dream may be like an acorn today. But someday it will grow to be like a mighty oak tree.

9b
Storms.

Even though you've decided to go for it and have your dream grow big and tall and strong, there's something else you need to know. Just like that mighty oak, there will be storms in your life. The oak tree doesn't come in to a hot supper and a nice warm bed every night. It's outside and has to face all types of weather. There may be freezing rain and high winds. Or maybe there will be hurricanes and tornadoes. An ice storm and a blizzard might come through. Whatever happens with the weather though, the oak tree must stand strong.

When I bend a big nail in half, it reminds me of how the oak tree has to be when it's in a storm. Just like the nail, the oak tree may bend but it never breaks. Then, when the storm is over (and, eventually, storms always leave), the oak tree can stand tall again. It's too tough to quit.

There will be challenges and hard times in your life. There will be storms. Life's not easy. But after every storm in your life, there will be a bright sunny day. If you let yourself break during the storm, you'll never experience the beautiful weather that follows. Sometimes you will definitely have to bend . . . just don't break.

affirmation #9b-

Even if I have to bend, I'll never break.

2 Boys and the ^{9c} Wise Old Lady.

Once upon a time in a small village, there lived a very wise old lady. She had become a legend in the region because she always had the right advice to give. Since she was very unselfish and really cared about people, the wise old lady would make herself available everyday. She would sit in the village square and answer people's questions. For several hours everyday, people from miles around would line up and have their problems solved.

Then one day, two teenage boys started hanging around. They watched and listened as the wise old lady encouraged and helped many, many people. They weren't impressed. In fact, the two boys became jealous of all the attention given to the wise old lady. These two boys, let's call them the wiseguys, decided to trick the wise old lady and make her look like a fool. As the two wiseguys were trying to figure out how to work their scam, one of them noticed a small bird on the ground. He picked it up and held it in his hand. The boy holding the bird said to his friend, "I've got it. I've got a way to trick the wise old lady. When I walk up to her, I'll have this little bird in my hands. I'll say, 'Wise old lady, wise old lady can you tell me if the bird in my hands is dead or alive?' If the wise old lady says that the bird is dead, I'll just open up my hands, the little bird will fly away and the wise old lady will be wrong. If she says that the bird is alive, I'll just crush the little bird and when I open my hands the bird will be dead. Either way, the wise old lady will be wrong and we'll have made her look like a fool."

The next day, the two wiseguys got up bright and early and went into the woods. They each found a little bird and held it gently in their hands. In fact, if you're reading this right now, I need you to make believe that you have a little bird in your hands. If may seem dumb, but do it anyway. Cup your hands and gently hold that little bird. Now, the two wiseguys got in line and went up to speak to the wise old lady. They stood in front of her and asked "Wise old lady, wise old lady can you tell us if the bird in our hands is dead or alive?" The boys were all excited because they thought that they were about to make the wise old lady look like a fool.

But the wise old lady just looked at them and smiled. She knew what they were trying to do. That's why she was the wise old lady. (Are you still holding your little bird?) She just looked at the two wiseguys and said, "The answer to that question is in your hands, it's your choice, it's up to you."

And that's what we've been talking about throughout this whole book. Choice. You have all the potential, all the possibilities, all the support, and all the ability that you need to do something really special with your life. But it comes down to your choice. Are you going to crush that little bird or let it fly? That little bird is your dream, it's all the great things that you could achieve in your life. You have something special to give the world and, in return, you'll have a joyful and rewarding life . . . if you choose wisely. Let that little bird live. Soar with the eagles.

It's been great sharing the wisdom in this book with you. We look forward to meeting you and hearing your story someday. We'll see you down the road. Be blessed . . . bye for now.

affirmation #9c-
My life, my choice.

Appendix a
Extra stuff.

I guess when you have some extra information, that doesn't really fit in with the rest of the story, it becomes an appendix. Since you're probably going to be in school for a few more years, this section can be very helpful. The information was shared with me many years ago by one of my favorite elevators, Dr. Rob Gilbert. It was so simple that I couldn't believe how powerful it was. It's called 'How to Become the World's Greatest Student.' Believe it or not, you don't need to be a rocket scientist in order to be a super student. But you do need to know the steps. There's only three and they're simple. Please note that simple is not always easy. The good news is that anyone can do the three steps. But just like the pledge, most kids refuse to believe . . . or they're too lazy . . . or they really don't want to do something special with their life.

The first step is called 'act as if.' This is all about having the right attitude and being in the right place. 'Act as if' you are the world's greatest student. What does a great student do? Come prepared for class. Sit in the front. Sit up straight. Look awake. Participate in class. Ask questions. Do neat work. Hand in assignments on time. Help others. Have a good attitude. That's it. That's the first step toward becoming a super student. Just like in the 'pledge' where you speak things about yourself that are going to be true, now you 'act as if' you're already a great student. If you've been a D student all your life, don't expect your grades to change overnight. But plant the 'act as if' seed now and it will grow into great grades later. And don't forget that school is really not about grades . . . it's about knowledge. Stay hungry to learn new stuff and you'll stay motivated in school. If you just stay focused on getting good grades, you'll probably get stressed out and school won't be fun. 'Act as if' you've got a great attitude and that you're hungry to learn as much as you can.

One of the major deterrents to your success in this step are crabs. When you attempt to do something special, the crabs will be looking to pull you back into the basket. Some kids will try to make you believe that being smart in school is not 'cool.' A lot of kids buy into this lie. They joke about being "dumb"or that they just don't care. The sad part is that, after you leave high school, most people only ever see about one out of every 100 kids that they went through school with. Yet so many kids waste years of their life worrying about what others think of them. Avoid this trap. Get the help you need, forget about what others say, and 'act as if.'

The second step is for you to get a dictionary and have it with you at all times. I know from personal experience that this is a very powerful step. When I was a kid, I developed some real bad habits. One of them was that I didn't read much. When I did read, I didn't really understand some of the words. Because I was lazy, I never took the time to look them up. I mean, if you asked me what a word meant, I could sort of tell you and maybe even use it in a sentence. I just didn't know the exact definition and that's important. So my grades were limited (to C's and D's) because my vocabulary was limited. Because of this, the colleges and universities that I wanted to attend didn't want me. I was fortunate enough to get into a small school and learn the secret. For four years, I carried a dictionary with me. Whenever I could not clearly define a word, out came the dictionary. In the beginning, this was a major pain. Sometimes it would take a long time just to read a sentence. But I knew that I was doing the right thing and I would pull out that dictionary every time.

The results were phenomenal. In my last three years of college, I received A's in every subject. Both of my parents fainted from the shock. After all the years of being a poor student, I was finally succeeding. I became hungry for knowledge and good grades just followed. All from a dictionary? Yes, and the patience to greatly improve my life. Have one with you at all times. Don't leave home without it.

The third step is just as simple as the others. Commit 2-3 hours everyday to improving yourself. Time actually in school doesn't count. You can include homework time. Just tell yourself, "Look, most kids are going to school, doing as little work as possible and then goofing off whenever they can. If I want to really be special, I'll need to do something different. If all it takes is a few hours a day, I'll go for it."

What if I get done with my homework at school or if I don't get any homework at all? What if there's no school? What about on weekends or summer vacations? The deal is everyday, 365 days per year. This is not punishment and it'll be a lot of fun. Have a bunch of great books lined up or get started on special projects for school or your community.

I know that this stuff works because it worked for me. If I could change from being a lazy, unmotivated, loser student to one of the 'world's greatest students,' so can you. Now that you have a plan for success, all you have to do is choose to start and then be 'too tough to quit.' The fun you'll have doing great things with your life will be a whole lot better than 'just hangin'.'

Appendix b

My **Pledge** to **Me**

from **Top Secrets of Success . . . 4 Kids.**

➤ I have a special gift inside me.

➤ I am a person of vision.

➤ I am excited about my dream. It gets clearer everyday.

➤ I was born to be great, but it can only happen if I seek the wisdom of the ages.

➤ I set goals for my life.

➤ I write down my goals. I do some work toward achieving my goals everyday.

➤ I seek quality mentors for my life. I have the strength to ask for help.

➤ I know that nothing can stop me, I persist through resistance.

➤ I build up, help, comfort, and encourage others at every opportunity.

➤ I am aware of the negative forces in my life. I face them.

➤ The real me is on the inside.

➤ Life's not easy. Challenges make me stronger.

➤ I have identified the things that are holding me back. I know the enemy.

➤ I make a move in faith to be courageous. I will crush the wall of negative in my life.

➤ I recognize and fight the little voice of negative in my mind.

➤ I will not compromise. I will run to my dreams, not from them.

➤ When it comes to my dream, I'm way above average.

➤ The red dragon has no power in my life. I've already won.

➤ I choose my friends carefully. I will not allow OPDs to steal my dream.

➤ I only trust my dreams to other dreamers.

➤ Bad seed yields bad fruit. I choose carefully.

➤ I take good care of the only body I will ever have.

➤ My life is valuable. I'm here for a reason. I don't take unnecessary chances.

- ➢ I don't need to smoke. I don't need to drink. I don't need drugs. Life gets me high.

- ➢ I plant good seed in my body. I take care of what my body needs.

- ➢ Garbage is not allowed near my computer, my brain.

- ➢ I treat others like I want to be treated. I give out good, so I know I'm gonna get good back.

- ➢ Tough times never last but tough people do. No one's allowed to put me down.

- ➢ I choose to be a positive person. I sow good seed.

- ➢ I overcome negative situations and feelings to reach my goals.

- ➢ The more I prepare, the more opportunities will come my way.

- ➢ The more I sweat in the books, the smarter I'll be on the street.

- ➢ In every adversity lies the seed of an equal or greater benefit (if I look for it). I'm too tough to quit.

- ➢ I always choose to do the right thing. My life is at stake.

- ➢ The way I speak will control the direction of my life.

- ➢ I control the direction of my life.

- ➢ My candle burns brightly. No one can extinguish my light.

➤ I have self-discipline. I make sure that the important things in my life get done.

➤ I pledge to take action. Great habits yield great results.

➤ I only speak good things about me . . . all the time.

➤ My life and my dream may be like an acorn today. But someday it will grow to be like a mighty oak tree.

➤ Even if I have to bend, I'll never break.

➤ My life, my choice.

Thanks. Some of these people are still around, some have gone home to be with the Lord (we hope). At some point, they were a huge help to us. They were either elevators or angels. Anyway, we're glad they showed up. In order of appearance:

Arlene & Frank Jones, Henry Dombrowski Sr., Stella & Henry Ziemski, Fran Vadimsky, Jane Izdebski, Gary Cook, Patty Kiefer, John Keilp Sr., Brother Patrick, Tom LaFronz, Dom Soricelli, Roy Weiss, Harry Brown, John Nasuta, Fred & Toni Lee Ponti, Steve & Roe Ribaudo, Bill Britt, Tommy White, Jesus Christ, Arne Larson, Tom Nuckel, Og Mandino, Nancy Dreher, Rosemary Farrell, Peggy Letsche, Mike Deasy, Bill Henderson, Mark Engler, Bill & Janet Higdon, Gene & Kay Putnam, Joyce Moore, Clarence McPeak, Rob Gilbert, Dennis Rogers, Tim Dreher, Gara Newman, Patti VanCauwenberg, Joe Pizzurro, Mario Perillo, Steve Perillo, Joe Licitra, Ron Chiricosta, Jules Edelman, Jo-Ann & Mitchell Ashkanazy, Andrew Bergman, Fred Marcus, Tom Bruinooge, Harry Flaherty, Bob Cangelosi, Joe Pompeo, Thomas & Julie Connelly, Sam Figueroa, Rick Kohler, Bill Giorgio, Gerard Gorman, John Sobecki, Maria Palumbo, Dottie Flanagan, Pete Ammerman, Mike Greenstein, Vic Boff, Slim the Hammerman, Mark Gibson, Pat Higgins, Paul & Glenda Anderson, Scott Magee, Pat Fiore.

If you've **read the book,**
if you're **doing the 'pledge,'**
if you're excited about who **YOU** are
and who **YOU** can become then it's time to . . .

Join the **Power Workshop Club**
and become a card-carryin' member . . .

Some of the benefits include:
   * your personal Power Workshop Club card.
   * special messages to keep you excited about YOUR dream.
   * discounts on bent nails, t-shirts, hats, tapes, other books,etc . . .
   * other stuff that we haven't even thought of yet . . .
   * and it's free . . .

Mail your request to the Power Workshop, 59 Upper Hibernia Road, Rockaway, NJ, 07866 or contact us through our website: **powerworkshop.org**

Russell Jones, husband and father of 4, has a background in education, business, fitness, and nutrition. Russell's wife and partner, **Lin,** is a mom, business-woman, cooking consultant, and a registered nurse. They bring their message of inspiration, motivation, and real self-esteem to thousands

of students, teachers and parents every year through their highly acclaimed Power Workshops.

• Notes •

• Notes •

• Notes •

• Notes •

• Notes •

• Notes •

• Notes •